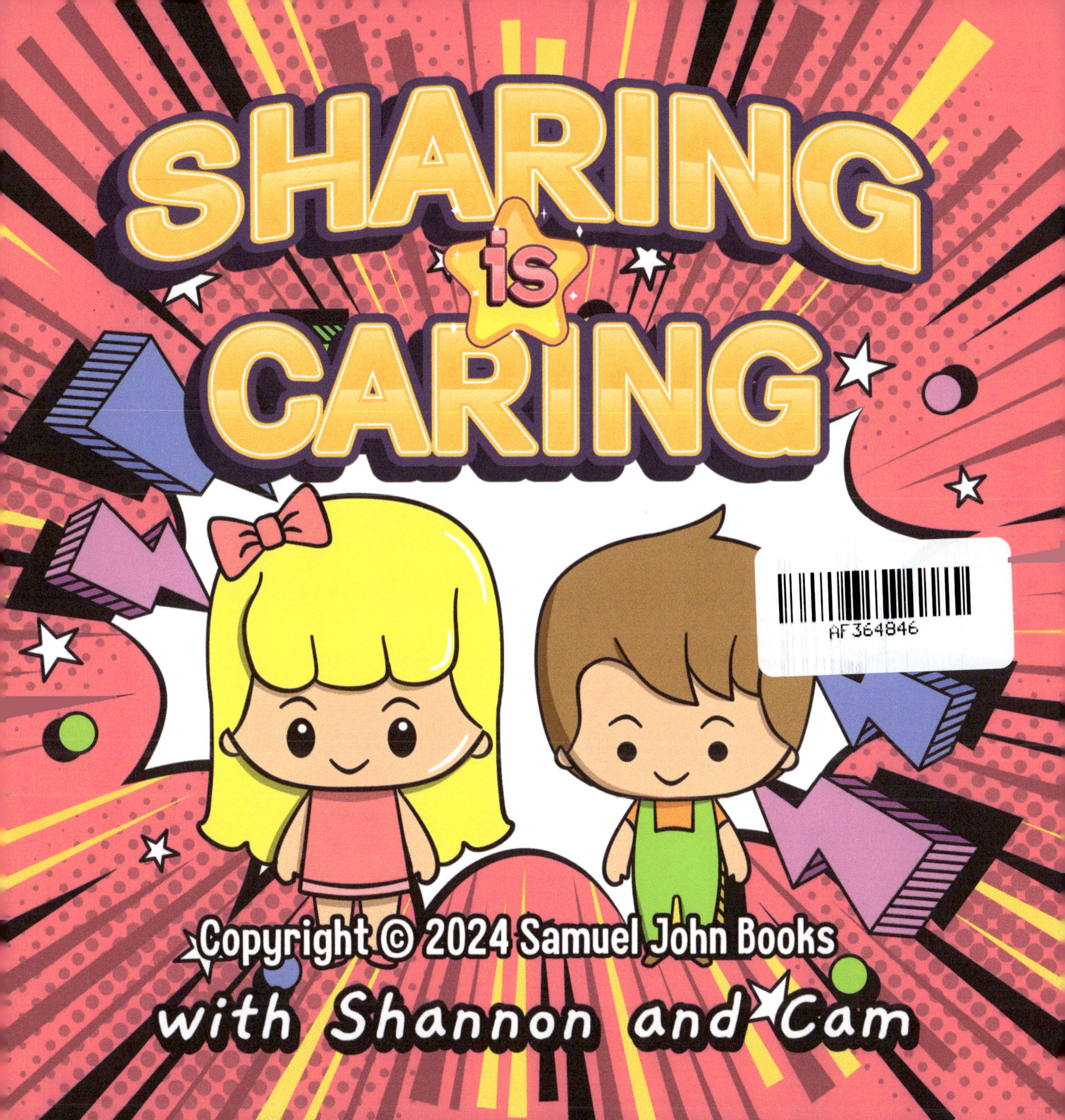

SHARING
IS
CARING
Copyright © 2024 Samuel John Books
with Shannon and Cam

Did you know that sharing is a great way to show someone how much you love them?

There is only one thing better than enjoying something that makes us smile, and that is sharing it with someone else. Two smiles are better than one!

Come and join Shannon and Cam on an adventure as you find out how sharing is caring!

When Shannon gets a cake on her birthday, she takes it to school to share a slice with all of her friends.

When Cam gets a new video game for Christmas, he invites his cousin over to play it with him.

When Shannon wins tickets to go to her favorite theme park, she asks her brother if he wants to go with her.

When Cam buys a big bag of sweets at lunchtime,
he offers some to his friend Josh.

In art class, there is only one box of crayons left. Shannon shares it with her friend Molly so they can both finish their own drawings.

When Cam plays with his ball in the garden, he comes up with a fun team game so everyone else can join in too.

When Molly drops her hot dog at the barbecue, Shannon chops hers in two and offers half to her best friend.

When Cam plays with his building blocks, he asks his sister if she wants to join in. Together, they make the tallest tower they have ever seen!

When Molly forgets her book at school, Shannon lets her friend sit next to her, and they read along together.

When the school holds a design competition, Cam decides to team up with his friend Josh because it's always more fun to work on something as a team.

When Shannon's clothes don't fit her anymore, she takes them to a charity shop so someone less fortunate can enjoy them.

When Cam plays soccer for the school team, he always passes to his teammates so everyone can join in with the game.

When Shannon went trick or treating, she got more candy than Molly. So, they decided to put all the candy into a big pile and split it in half.

When Mom and Dad volunteer at the food bank to serve dinner to homeless people, Cam always goes along to help.

When Shannon and Cam watch a movie at home, they always share the popcorn.

Cam is very good at math, but Josh sometimes struggles. So Cam always takes the time to teach his friend how to do the hard sums

When there is only one ice cream left in the freezer, Shannon always shares it with her brother.

When Mom and Dad aren't looking, Cam even shares some of his dinner with the dog!

Creating a checklist of sharing actions is a great idea to encourage positive social behavior. Here is a checklist you can do:

- [ ] **Sharing Toys:** Did I share my toys with friends or siblings?
- [ ] **Offering Help:** Did I offer to help someone who needed it?
- [ ] **Inviting Others to Play:** Did I include others in games and activities?
- [ ] **Sharing Snacks or Treats:** Did I offer to share my snacks or treats with friends or siblings?
- [ ] **Helping Someone in Need:** Did I offer help to someone who was struggling or upset?
- [ ] **Sharing Knowledge or Skills:** Did I help someone learn something new that I am good at?
- [ ] **Sharing the Spotlight:** Did I let others have a chance to be in the spotlight or lead activities?
- [ ] **Sharing Craft Supplies:** Did I share my craft supplies like crayons, paper, or scissors with others?

Help Shannon get to Molly to share her birthday cake with her

And here it ends!

We hope you liked it and learned new things.

Goodbye! Until next time!

I want to ask you a favor so that this book reaches more people, and that is that you rate it with a sincere opinion on the platform where you purchased it.

With that small gesture, you will be helping me to carry on with new projects.

I can't wait to start creating my next book for you!

See you soon!

LEARN WITH OUR
EDUCATIONAL CHILDREN'S BOOKS

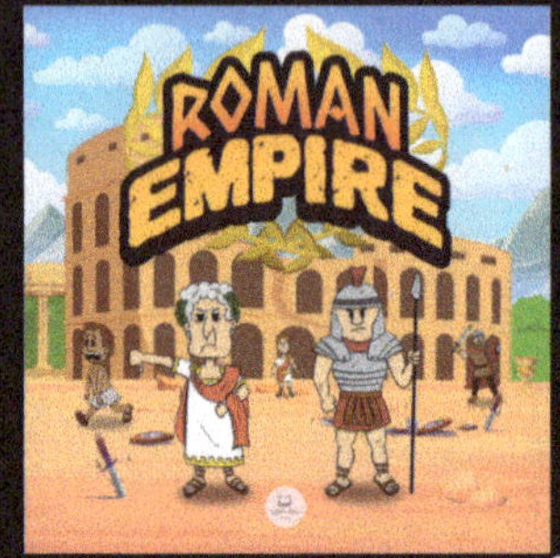

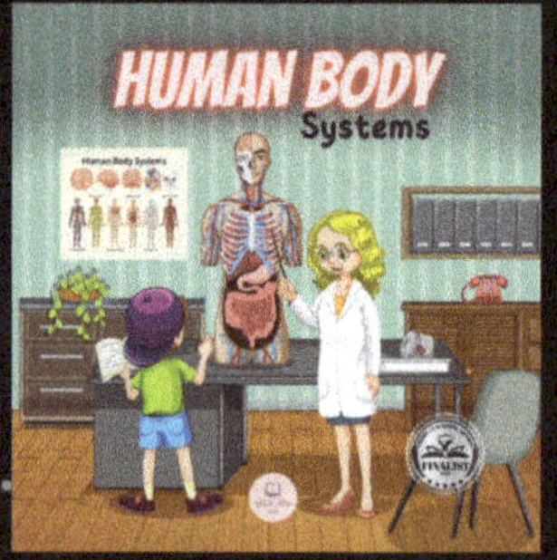

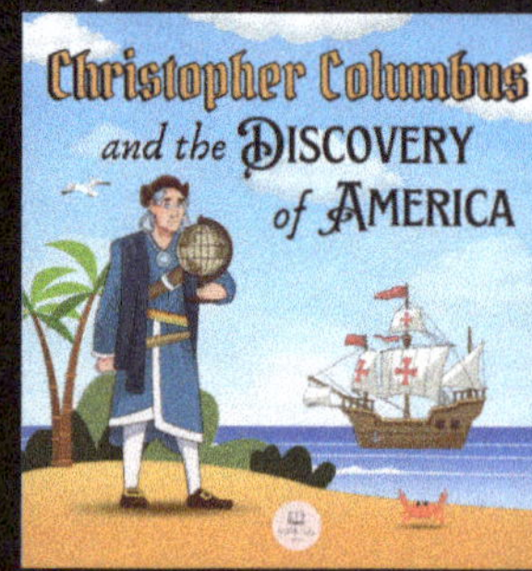

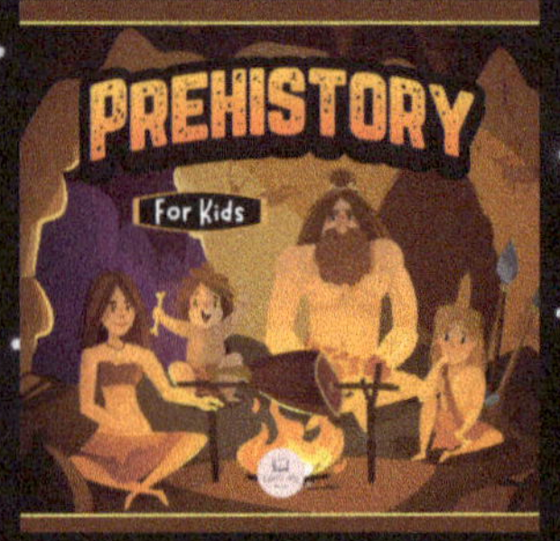

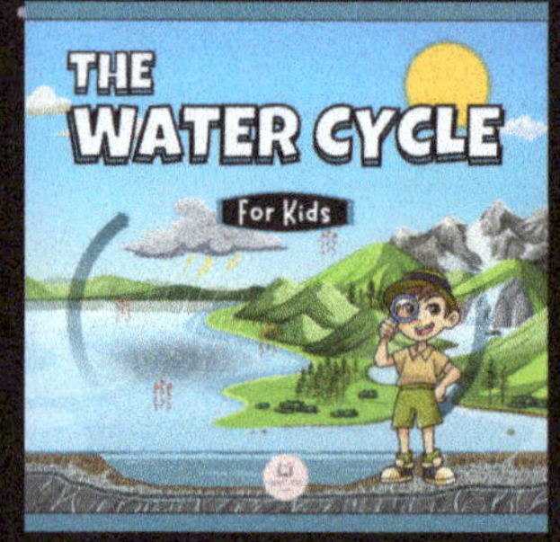

https://www.pge.me/childrensbooks

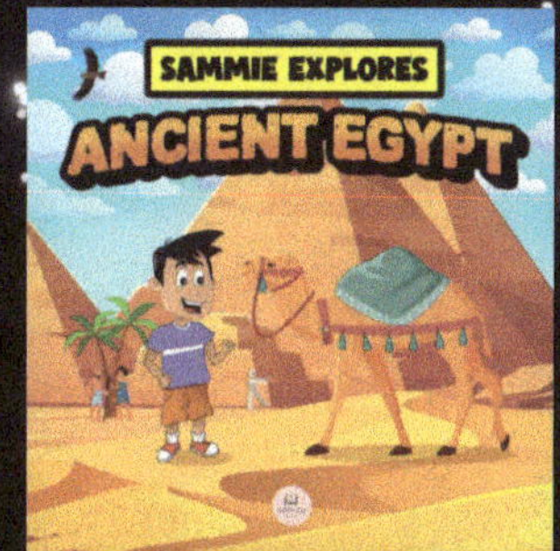

www.pge.me/childrensbooks

contacto@samueljohnbooks.com

www.facebook.com/bookssamueljohn/

www.amazon.com/author/samueljohnbooks

Subscribe to my newsletter, receive 4 FREE BONUS, and stay informed of new publications, offers, and promotions of free books.

www.subscribepage.io/ebookfree

Bonus #1 - Free ebook "The The Steadfast Tin Soldier"
Bonus #2 - 19 Printable Halloween Coloring Pages
Bonus #3 - 50 Printable Mazes With Solutions
Bonus #4 - Free ebook With Sample Pages